D1384862

WOLF SPIDERS

by Josh Gregory

Children's Press®

An Imprint of Scholastic Inc.
New York   Toronto   London   Auckland   Sydney
Mexico City   New Delhi   Hong Kong
Danbury, Connecticut

Content Consultant
Dr. Stephen S. Ditchkoff
Professor of Wildlife Sciences
Auburn University
Auburn, Alabama

Photographs © 2014: age fotostock/tdietrich: 4, 5 background, 19;
Alamy Images/Danita Delimont: 32; AP Images/The Tennessean,
Mandy Lunn: 36; Bob Italiano: 44 foreground, 45 foreground;
Dreamstime: 27 (Cathy Keifer), 2 background, 3, 44 background,
45 background (Kiankhoon); Media Bakery: 24 (Bartomeu Borrell),
35 (Frans Lanting), 5 top, 12 (Paul E. Tessier); Science Source: 15,
20 (ANT Photo Library), 8, 23 (Francesco Tomasinelli), 31 (John
Mitchell), 1, 7, 46 (Millard H. Sharp), 28 (Samuel Zschokke);
Shutterstock, Inc./Cathy Keifer: cover, 11; Superstock, Inc.: 5 bottom,
16 (Matthias Lenke/F1 ONLINE), 2 foreground, 39, 40 (NHPA).

Library of Congress Cataloging-in-Publication Data
Gregory, Josh.
 Wolf spiders / by Josh Gregory.
 pages cm.—(Nature's children)
 Audience: 9–12.
 Audience: Grade 4 to 6.
 Includes bibliographical references and index.
 ISBN 978-0-531-23363-4 (lib. bdg.) — ISBN 978-0-531-25161-4 (pbk.)
 1. Wolf spiders—Juvenile literature. I. Title.
 QL458.42.L9G74 2013
 595.4'8—dc23   2013000096

No part of this publication may be reproduced in whole or in part,
or stored in a retrieval system, or transmitted in any form or by any
means, electronic, mechanical, photocopying, recording, or otherwise,
without written permission of the publisher. For information regarding
permission, write to Scholastic Inc., Attention: Permissions Department,
557 Broadway, New York, NY 10012.
© 2014 Scholastic Inc.

All rights reserved. Published in 2014 by Children's Press, an imprint
of Scholastic Inc.

Printed in China 62
SCHOLASTIC, CHILDREN'S PRESS, and associated logos are
trademarks and/or registered trademarks of Scholastic Inc.

1 2 3 4 5 6 7 8 9 10 R 23 22 21 20 19 18 17 16 15 14

Wolf Spiders

Class	Arachnida
Order	Araneae
Family	Lycosidae
Genera	120
Species	2,388
World distribution	Worldwide
Habitats	Any land environment where insects are found
Distinctive physical characteristics	Eight legs; eight eyes arranged in three rows; strong, venomous fangs; generally colored to provide camouflage in natural habitats; species vary widely in size; females are usually larger than males
Habits	Active predators; fast runners; many species create burrows in the ground; mothers carry egg sacs until they are ready to hatch, then carry newly hatched babies on their backs for several days
Diet	Mostly eat insects and other spiders; large species sometimes eat small reptiles and amphibians

Contents

CHAPTER 1

A Natural Hunter

Deep in the woods of a South Carolina forest, a dangerous **predator** emerges from its underground home. It stalks through the undergrowth in search of a meal. Hidden in the darkness, the fearsome hunter uses its eyes to scan the grassy forest floor. As it moves its hairy body along the ground, it keeps a careful watch over its surroundings, in case any larger animals decide to make a snack of it.

Finally, this Carolina wolf spider, the largest wolf spider **species** found in North America, spots an unlucky insect in the grass ahead. The dangerous killer springs forward with a sudden burst of speed and easily overtakes its **prey**. Holding the insect down with its **pedipalps**, the triumphant hunter sinks its fangs into its victim and begins to eat.

There are around 2,400 different species of wolf spiders living today. They are found in almost all land environments on the planet.

A fully grown Carolina wolf spider has a leg span of 3 to 4 inches (7.6 to 10.1 centimeters).

Hunting Down Dinner

Most species of spiders spin webs to capture prey. Wolf spiders aren't like most other spiders, though. Instead of waiting around for prey to get stuck in the sticky threads of a web, these amazing arachnids leave their homes at night to hunt down their targets. They are called wolf spiders because they use hunting methods that are a lot like the ones wolves use. When prey wanders near, a wolf spider will chase after it and leap onto its back. It then bites quickly, poisoning the prey with its venom.

Wolf spiders eat almost anything they can catch and kill. Because they are fairly small, they mostly eat insects and other small invertebrates. However, wolf spiders are not afraid to attack animals that are slightly larger than they are.

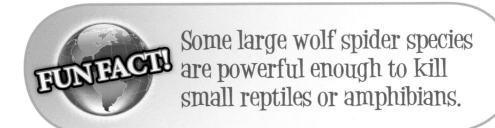

FUN FACT! Some large wolf spider species are powerful enough to kill small reptiles or amphibians.

A grasshopper is just one of the many options on a wolf spider's menu.

A Closer Look

Even though they seem small to us, some wolf spider species are large compared to most other types of spiders. The largest are about 1.2 inches (3 centimeters) long. Female wolf spiders are usually larger than males. However, not all wolf spiders are quite so big. In fact, the smallest wolf spiders have bodies that are around 0.1 inches (2.5 mm) long. This is smaller than many other common spiders, including the dangerous brown recluse.

Like all spiders, wolf spiders are invertebrates. This means they lack a spine or internal skeleton. Instead, they have hardened outer bodies called exoskeletons. These bodies are divided into two sections, with four legs attached to each one.

The front body section is called the cephalothorax. It holds the spider's mouth, stomach, brain, and eyes. A wolf spider's pedipalps are also attached to the cephalothorax. Pedipalps are like small legs. The spider can use them to hold down prey or to feel ahead of itself.

Adult male
6 ft. (1.8 m)

Wolf spider
1.2 in (3 cm)

A male spider's pedipalps are larger than a female's.

What's on the Inside

A spider's rear body section is known as its abdomen. This is where most of its internal organs, such as its stomach and lungs, are located. A spider's circulatory system is much simpler than the type found in humans and most other large animals. In large animals, blood is transported throughout the body using a series of tubes. The spider's heart simply pumps blood into open areas surrounding its internal organs.

A spider's respiratory system is also very different from the one humans have. Each spider has two sets of book lungs. These lungs get their name because they are made up of thin structures that look like book pages. The "pages" are exposed to air, taking in oxygen. Wolf spiders also get oxygen from tubes called tracheae. Tracheae lead directly from the inside of the spider's abdomen to holes in the exoskeleton. As air flows in through the holes, the spider's body absorbs oxygen. The air then flows back out.

Spiders do not breathe air in and out the way people do. Instead, air is pushed in and out of their bodies as they move around.

Digging a Den

Wolf spiders are most common in grassy areas such as fields. This is because they mainly feed and survive on the ground, crawling through grass or under rocks and logs. Some wolf spiders make homes in these locations. They live under rocks, logs, or even underneath the bark of trees. Only a few species are known to climb up into taller plants.

Most wolf spiders burrow underground to build dens. Some dens are long, deep tubes. Others are shallow and bowl-shaped. Many wolf spiders line their burrows with the same silk that other spiders use to spin webs. They produce this silk in their bodies and release it through spinnerets. The silk becomes strong and hard as it dries. Lining their dens with silk helps secure the walls and entrance of the burrow, preventing collapses. Some wolf spiders cover the entrances to their dens using leaves, grass, and other materials. Others build up small walls around the entrance to help keep it hidden.

Wolf spiders build their burrows wherever they can find a safe, hidden location.

CHAPTER 2

Spider Survival

Wolf spiders have a range of powerful senses to help them hunt for prey and avoid threats. Vision is one of the most important of these senses. Wolf spiders can see better than most other spiders. A wolf spider's eight eyes are arranged in three rows: four in front, two in the middle, and two in the back. The front eyes are smallest, and the ones in the center are largest. This arrangement is one of the ways that experts can tell wolf spiders apart from other kinds of spiders.

Wolf spiders also rely heavily on touch. They can feel the slightest vibrations in the ground as organisms around them move. Their bodies are covered in tiny hairs that sense vibrations in the air, which allows them to detect sound. This can alert the spiders to approaching predators or other threats.

A spider's body hairs vary in length and are water repellent.

Masters of Mobility

Thanks to their eight strong legs, spiders are very good at moving across a variety of surfaces. They can walk not only along flat surfaces but also up plants, walls, or anything else they need to climb. This is because each of their legs ends in a thick covering of incredibly tiny hairs. Each of these hairs has a textured, foot-shaped end that allows it to grip almost any surface. In addition, a spider's legs are divided into seven segments, making them very flexible. This flexibility enables the spider to step carefully across uneven surfaces or take steps up onto higher ledges.

While all spiders are noted for their mobility, wolf spiders are especially fast. This speed comes in handy when the spiders are chasing down their prey.

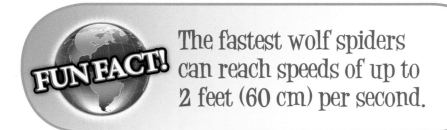

FUN FACT! The fastest wolf spiders can reach speeds of up to 2 feet (60 cm) per second.

The gripping hairs on the bottom of a spider's leg are called scopular hairs.

Predators Become Prey

Because of their relatively small size, wolf spiders have to defend themselves from many predators. Larger spiders can be a threat. So can insects such as praying mantises and wasps. Certain types of ants can group together to kill wolf spiders. In addition, the spiders must watch out for larger animals such as reptiles, amphibians, and birds.

A wolf spider's best defense is to stay out of sight. One way the spiders do this is by staying in their burrows when they are not attacking prey. They also rely on camouflage. A wolf spider's body is usually colored to blend in with its natural surroundings. Because wolf spiders live on the ground, most species are shades of brown or black. Many species have stripes, spots, and other markings that make them harder to notice.

Because they are fast, wolf spiders can sometimes flee if they come face-to-face with predators. They will attempt to bite their enemies only if left with no option for escape.

It can be very difficult to spot a well-camouflaged spider, like this wolf spider.

CHAPTER 3

From Hatchling to Adult

Wolf spiders do not often spend a lot of time together. Adults always live and hunt alone. Some species are comfortable living near fellow wolf spiders, while others are territorial. One of the only situations in which adult wolf spiders are sure to be in each other's company is when it comes time for them to mate.

The mating process begins when a male wolf spider works to attract a female. He communicates his readiness to mate mainly using visual signals. For example, many species move their pedipalps in a special pattern. They also tap their legs, pedipalps, and bodies on the ground to produce vibrations. The female feels these small vibrations in the sensitive hairs that cover her body and knows that a potential mate is nearby. During the mating process, the male fertilizes the female's eggs, making them ready to be laid.

Female wolf spiders sometimes eat males after mating.

Mother Knows Best

After mating, a female wolf spider lays a clutch of several dozen eggs. She then spins silk and uses it to bundle the eggs together in a round sac. Most types of spiders leave their egg sacs in a safe place and go on with their lives at this point. Female wolf spiders, on the other hand, keep close watch over their egg sacs. A mother wolf spider attaches her egg sac to her spinnerets and carries it with her wherever she goes.

When it is time for the eggs to hatch, the mother bites a small hole in the outside of the sac to let her babies out. The newborn wolf spiders look like tiny versions of their parents. They immediately climb onto their mother's back after hatching. The babies ride along with her for several days before striking out on their own.

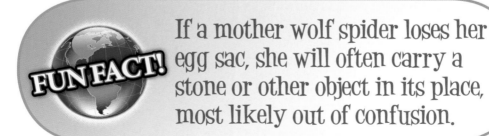

FUN FACT! If a mother wolf spider loses her egg sac, she will often carry a stone or other object in its place, most likely out of confusion.

A single wolf spider mother can carry hundreds of newly hatched babies on her body.

Growing and Changing

Because spiders have exoskeletons instead of soft outer skins, they grow through a process called **molting**. The spider grows a new, larger exoskeleton beneath the old one. First, the spider's body absorbs the bottom layer of the old exoskeleton and uses it as a base for growing a new one. It releases fluid in between the old and new exoskeletons as the new one grows.

Because the new, larger exoskeleton is inside a smaller one, it folds up as it grows. When the spider is ready to shed its old skin, its body reabsorbs the fluid between the two layers. This leaves a space between the layers. The spider's body then increases blood flow in the cephalothorax beneath the new exoskeleton. The new exoskeleton unfolds and cracks the old one. Finally, the spider moves and flexes its muscles until the old exoskeleton is completely removed. Molting happens often when the spider is young and becomes less common as it ages.

A spider's exoskeleton does not stretch as the spider grows larger.

CHAPTER 4

The Family Web

Spiders have roamed the planet for hundreds of millions of years. Though many of these ancient species are long extinct, scientists are still learning about them today. They do this by studying the fossils that ancient spiders left behind. Fossils can help scientists learn when different spider species first appeared, their size, and even what they ate.

To date, the largest spider fossil that scientists have discovered is of the species *Nephila jurassica*. This spider was around 1 inch (2.5 cm) long, with legs extending 2.5 inches (6.4 cm). The species dates back to at least 165 million years ago. Because of the spinnerets on the spider's legs, scientists believe that it spun large, strong webs.

Sometimes scientists find fossils not just of a spider's body but also of its web. One of the oldest web fossils ever found dates back around 110 million years. The fossilized web had several insect bodies trapped in it, providing clues to the ancient spider's diet.

Fossilized threads of spider silk provide scientists with important clues about wolf spider ancestors.

Towering Tarantulas

There are around 42,700 different spider species living today. One type that is closely related to wolf spiders is the tarantula. There are around 900 tarantula species. Some of them are extremely large. The Goliath bird-eating spider is the largest known spider. This terrifying spider's leg span can grow to be 12 inches (30 cm) wide. That is about as wide as an average dinner plate!

Like wolf spiders, tarantulas do not rely on webs to catch their prey. Some species actively hunt, while others hide and wait for unsuspecting prey to get close. Tarantulas kill their prey with the help of their venomous fangs, just as wolf spiders do. Some tarantulas use their silk to attach trip lines to their home burrows. When prey animals touch the lines, it sends vibrations into the burrow. This lets the tarantula know that a tasty snack is near.

Goliath bird-eating spiders live up to their name by hunting and eating birds.

Close Cousins

Nursery web spiders are another close relative of wolf spiders. They look so similar to wolf spiders that the two types are often mistaken for each other. Like wolf spiders, nursery web spiders take special care of their young. Mother nursery web spiders carry their egg sacs just like wolf spiders do. However, instead of carrying the sacs in their spinnerets, they carry them in their jaws. The mother hides her egg sac under a web of leaves when the babies are ready to hatch. She then guards the area until the spiderlings are safe and ready to leave the hidden nest. This process gives the nursery web spider its name.

Wolf spiders are also related to the deadly brown recluse. Because wolf spiders and brown recluses can look similar, people often confuse them. The brown recluse is one of the most poisonous spiders in the world. Its bite can cause serious wounds and has even been known to kill people who are small.

When it is time for nursery web spiders to hatch, the mother opens a hole in her egg sac to let the babies out.

All About Arachnids

Spiders belong to a larger class of animals called arachnids. Another common type of arachnid is the scorpion. Scorpions are similar to spiders in many ways. They have eight legs and hard exoskeletons. However, a scorpion would not be mistaken for a spider. A scorpion's pedipalps are much larger than a spider's, and they end in large pincers. Scorpions also have long tails that curl up over their backs. These tails end in venomous stingers that scorpions use to kill prey and attack enemies.

Another well-known arachnid is the daddy longlegs. Many people think that daddy longlegs are spiders because of how they look. However, daddy longlegs only have one body section instead of the separate cephalothorax and abdomen that spiders have.

Other arachnids include tiny mites and ticks. Most mite and tick species are parasites. They live by attaching themselves to larger animals. Some mite species, however, live on a diet of plants.

There are around 1,500 different scorpion species.

CHAPTER 5

Living Side by Side with Spiders

Wolf spiders can look very intimidating. Because some spiders are so dangerous, many people are scared of all spiders they see. However, wolf spiders are much more helpful than they are harmful to people. They never attack or bite a human unless someone tries to pick them up. When they do bite, the venom is not strong enough to cause any serious damage. A bite from a large wolf spider is about as painful as a bee sting.

Because they are such skilled hunters, wolf spiders are a big help in keeping insect populations in check. This is especially necessary in areas where too many of a certain insect species can cause major problems for people. For example, some insects eat farmers' crops. An overly large population of these species can destroy entire fields. But with a healthy wolf spider population in the area, it is less likely that the insects will grow too numerous.

It is dangerous to handle wolf spiders, but perfectly safe to observe them.

Homeless Hunters

No wolf spider species are currently endangered. However, they are still facing a major threat. As human populations continue to grow, people need more space and natural resources to maintain their way of life. This often comes at the expense of natural environments. People clear away plants to make room for homes, businesses, and farmland. This changes the habitat, so wolf spiders and other animals are left with fewer places to live and hunt. As a result, populations of wolf spiders and other species decrease. The spiders might also end up living in crop fields or buildings rather than their familiar forest home.

The only way to solve this problem is to protect our natural environments. Read about ways you can help protect forests and other habitats near your home and around the world. You can also talk to your parents, teachers, and other adults about ways to become more involved. Remember to always respect even the smallest wild animals.

Wolf spiders might seem small, but they still need
plenty of space to live and hunt in the wild.

Being a Good Neighbor

Because they live in burrows, wolf spiders rarely end up inside buildings. When they do, though, treat them with respect. Remember that they help get rid of pesky insects. Try using a stick to guide the spider into a jar or other container, and then set it free outdoors.

Before you set the spider free, you might try keeping it as a pet for a few days. Because wolf spiders do not build webs, they do not need much space to live. Keep your new pet in a safe container, such as a clean jar with holes in the lid. Be sure to catch insects for it to eat, usually one a day. You can also buy crickets from some pet stores. Watching the spider can help you learn about the way it lives. After a few days, release it outside. In its natural home, it can play its part in keeping the ecosystem balanced. It's a big job, but this fierce hunter has what it takes.

Like all wild animals, wolf spiders deserve respect from humans.

Words to Know

arachnids (uh-RAK-nidz) — a class of animals that includes spiders, scorpions, daddy longlegs, ticks, and mites

camouflage (KAM-uh-flahzh) — a disguise or a natural coloring that allows animals, people, or objects to hide by making them look like their surroundings

circulatory system (SIR-kyuh-luh-tor-ee SIS-tuhm) — the group of organs that pump blood through the body

class (KLAS) — a scientific classification that groups together similar orders of life forms

clutch (KLUHCH) — a nest of eggs

ecosystem (EE-koh-sis-tuhm) — all the living things in a place and their relation to the environment

endangered (en-DAYN-jurd) — at risk of becoming extinct, usually because of human activity

extinct (ik-STINGKT) — no longer found alive; known about only through fossils or history

fertilizes (FUR-tuh-ly-ziz) — joins sperm cells with eggs from a female

fossils (FAH-suhlz) — bones, shells, or other traces of animals or plants from millions of years ago, preserved as rock

invertebrates (in-VUR-tuh-brits) — animals without a backbone

mate (MATE) — to join together to produce babies

molting (MOHLT-ing) — losing old fur, feathers, exoskeleton, or skin so that new ones can grow

organs (OR-guhnz) — parts of the body

parasites (PAR-uh-sites) — animals or plants that live on or inside another animal or plant

pedipalps (PEH-duh-palps) — small arms near the jaws that help a spider dig, move, and hold on to food

predator (PRED-uh-tur) — an animal that lives by hunting other animals for food

prey (PRAY) — an animal that's hunted by another animal for food

respiratory system (RES-pur-uh-tor-ee SIS-tuhm) — a system of organs functioning in respiration and in humans consisting especially of the nose, nasal passages, pharynx, larynx, trachea, bronchi, and lungs

sac (SAK) — a bag or pouchlike structure that a spider uses to hold a clutch of eggs

species (SPEE-sheez) — one of the groups into which animals and plants of the same genus are divided; members of the same species can mate and have offspring

spinnerets (spin-uh-RETS) — organs for producing threads of silk from the secretion of silk glands

territorial (terr-uh-TOR-ee-uhl) — defensive of a certain area

venom (VEN-uhm) — poison produced by some spiders, snakes, and insects; venom is usually passed into a victim's body through a bite or sting

Habitat Map

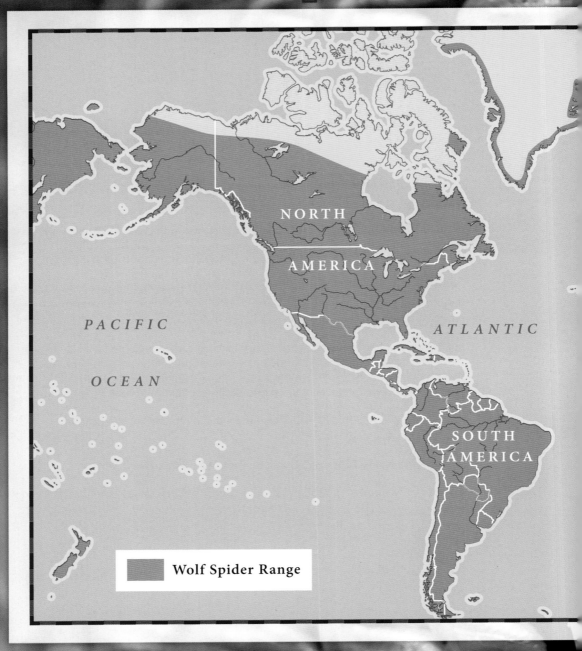

NORTH
AMERICA

SOUTH
AMERICA

PACIFIC

OCEAN

ATLANTIC

Wolf Spider Range

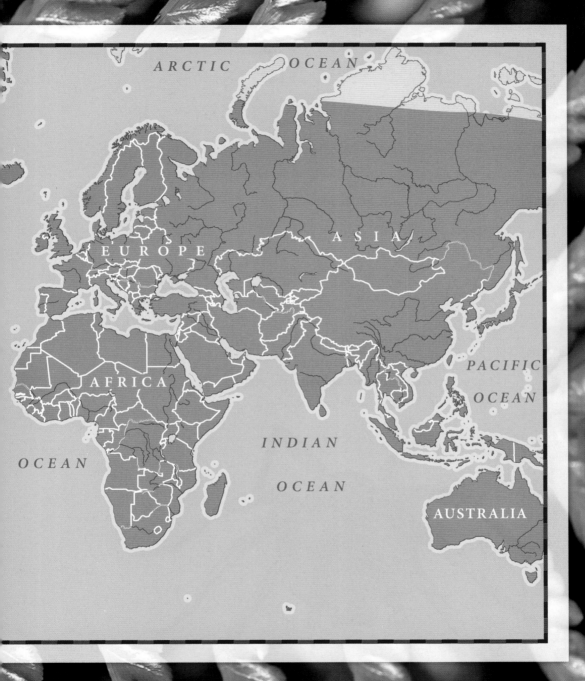

ARCTIC OCEAN

ASIA

EUROPE

AFRICA

PACIFIC OCEAN

OCEAN

INDIAN

OCEAN

AUSTRALIA

Find Out More

Books

Hibbert, Clare. *Spiders*. Mankato, MN: Arcturus, 2011.

Markle, Sandra. *Wolf Spiders: Mothers on Guard*. Minneapolis: Lerner, 2011.

McLeese, Don. *Spiders*. Vero Beach, FL: Rourke, 2012.

Morgan, Sally. *Spiders*. Mankato, MN: Amicus, 2011.

Visit this Scholastic Web site for more information on wolf spiders:
www.factsfornow.scholastic.com
Enter the keywords **Wolf Spiders**

Index

Page numbers in *italics* indicate a photograph or map.

About the Author

Josh Gregory writes and edits books for kids. He lives in Chicago, Illinois.